How to Get Rid of
BAD DREAMS

Nancy Hazbry
Roy Condy

SCHOLASTIC INC.

New York Toronto London Auckland Sydney

For my mother, and for my son Bryan,
who had the dreams
                    Nancy Hazbry

For Elizabeth
                    Roy Condy

ISBN 0-590-43474-8

Copyright © 1983 by Nancy Hazbry and Roy Condy.
All rights reserved. Published by Scholastic Inc.,
730 Broadway, New York, NY 10003, by arrangement with
Scholastic - TAB Publications.

12 11 10 9 8 7 6 5 4 3   0 1 2 3 4 5/9

Printed in the U.S.A.   08
First Scholastic printing, April 1990

Did you ever dream you were being chased by a scary ghost uttering horrible moans and groans? Sometimes bad dreams can make you afraid. But there are ways to make bad dreams and scary monsters go away.

Here is the secret...

If you dream you are being chased down a lonely road by a bunch of ugly monsters with pointy horns and jagged teeth and terrible claws, don't worry.

All you have to do is...

take a mirror out of your pocket and hold it in front of them. When the monsters see themselves, they will be so scared they'll turn around and run the other way.

If you dream you are walking in the park
on a sunny afternoon when a huge dragon jumps
out at you from behind a bush and tries to fry you
with his fiery breath, don't worry.

All you have to do is...

pull your shrink-ray laser
out of your belt and fire until the
dragon shrivels to the size of a kitten.
Then you can be the only one in school with
your own pet dragon.

If you dream you get lost in a jungle and step
into quicksand up to your waist, and every move
just makes you sink deeper and deeper, don't worry.

All you have to do is...

take off your hat and have a sip
from the bottle of reducing potion in your
knapsack. Soon you will be small enough to fit
in your hat and you can row to safety.

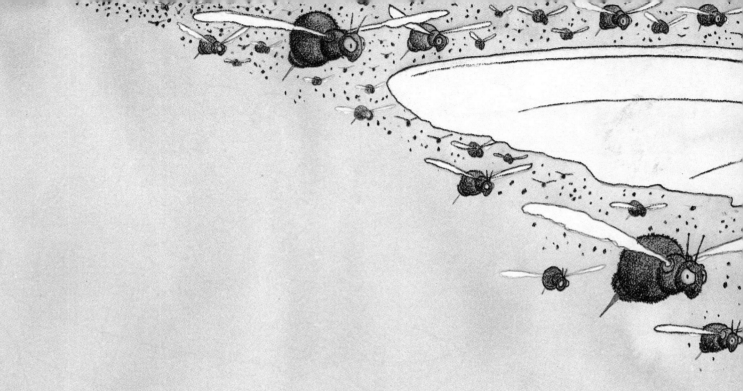

If you dream you are being attacked by
one-hundred-and-ninety-nine billion black, scary,
hairy bugs with green eyes and red stingers, don't worry.

All you have to do is...

whip out a can of silver paint and spray it all
over the bugs, then take a deep breath and blow
them into the sky. That will make one-hundred-
and-ninety-nine billion new glittering stars.

If you dream you are just sitting down to lunch
after climbing the highest mountain in the world,
and suddenly a fierce wind starts to blow you
right over the edge into a bottomless crevice,
and you have dropped your pick,
and your rope is getting frayed,
don't worry.

All you have to do is...

chew six pieces of really sticky bubble gum, stick a great wad on the bottom of each foot and walk back down the mountain.

If you dream that a warty, bristly, ugly troll
captures you and laughs at all your efforts
to escape, don't worry.

All you have to do is...

laugh right back at him, as loud and as long as you can. Soon you won't know why you were so scared of him, and you might even become friends.

If you dream you are trapped inside a giant's nose
and it's dark and you can't find your way out,
don't worry.

All you have to do is reach for your flashlight
and — Oh, no! You've dropped it!

Hold on, don't worry.

All you have to do is...

borrow a feather from your pet parrot and tickle
the inside of the giant's nose. He'll sneeze
so hard he'll blow you right out. Then use your
umbrella as a parachute to float safely down
to earth.

If you dream that

a scary ghost uttering horrible moans and groans,
a bunch of ugly monsters with pointy horns and jagged teeth and
    terrible claws,
a huge dragon with fiery breath,
one-hundred-and-ninety-nine billion scary, hairy bugs with
    green eyes and red stingers,
and a warty, bristly troll
are chasing you, and you are stuck
in bottomless quicksand in the jungle,
in a fierce wind at the top of the highest mountain in the world,
or in the dark inside a giant's nose,
and if you can't figure out what to do, don't worry.

All you have to do is...

grab your teddy bear, and your blanket, and your
older sister or brother, and your dog or cat,
then run like mad and jump into bed with Mummy or
Daddy or Grandma or Grampa. Then snuggle deep under
the soft, warm covers

...and have sweet dreams!